Surviving Doomsday: Techniques to Help You Survive After a Bio Attack

JD Everman

Warning

The survival techniques and medical advice contained within this book are for extreme survival circumstances. Any misuse of advice that results in damage, loss or bodily harm is not the responsibility of the publisher or author. Please use common sense and seek a medical professional whenever possible. When practicing survival techniques, observe all laws protecting any particular species of plant in your region.

Please also respect any local or federal laws and ordinances when considering practicing techniques outlined in this book. The following chapters are meant for educational purposes only. In no way do we advocate anyone breaking the law, and we cannot be held responsible for the actions of readers.

Performance of techniques outlined in this book is done at your own risk.

Stay safe always.

Table of Contents

Introduction

Surviving Doomsday is all about necessary techniques and tips to help you prepare for an attack. It is assumed that you already own, or will act to acquire, many of the suggested items. Failure to prepare far in advance of a disaster actually taking place will only serve to invalidate the following techniques. Listed in this text are beneficial items, tips, storage techniques, and survival advice to help you plan for the worst.

This book was specifically written to help people prepare for biological attacks. The unfortunate truth of the matter is that someday, you will need to know how to defend your loved ones when an attack occurs and you are left without law-enforcement or local government entities to keep you safe. When and if this happens, there are basic skills that everyone needs to have in order to ensure survival. Without basic survival techniques, your chances of living more than a few weeks at most after an attack occurs are drastically reduced.

While this book is geared towards surviving after a biological attack takes place, there are plenty of skills inside these pages that can be used on a day-to-day basis. In the following chapters, techniques, tips and methods are outlined to ensure that you will have the ability to identify what a pandemic is, when it has occurred, and how to defend yourself against it.

You will learn basic food storage techniques, how to know when a pandemic strikes your area, and much more. Suggestions on home defense, including weaponry, are also included. You'll even read some suggestions geared around what to do should you be forced to flee your home in order to stay alive. Don't allow yourself to exist without the necessary skills required to survive should a biological attack occur in your area. Make sure that you take the steps required to keep you and your loved ones as safe as humanly possible.

Do you have what it takes to survive doomsday?

Identifying Biological Attacks

Exactly what is a pandemic? To put it briefly, a pandemic is any infectious disease that has spread through the human population across a large region. This could be across multiple continents, or the disease can be spread worldwide. This is much different than an *endemic*, which is any infectious disease that is stable in terms of the number of people getting sick from it. A pandemic can come from a biological attack, or it can be spread through natural means. Many, many years ago, Native Americans were subjected to a variety of diseases when they came in contact with settlers. The settlers carried antibodies that the Native Americans did not yet possess. The end result was widespread sickness throughout the land.

While that is an example of a pandemic being caused by natural means, the possibility of a biological attack is still great. In fact, the outlook grows grimmer with each passing day. With the rise of new technologies and weaponized viruses, we must take steps to protect ourselves more now than ever before.

How does one identify when a biological or chemical attack has happened in their area? There are several steps that you can take to know whether or not something like this has occurred. Firstly, stay on the lookout for dead animals. This includes birds, fish, or any other wild animal. Be on the lookout especially for smaller animals in the wild. If you begin to see a large number of dead animals spread across the same area, that's a huge red flag.

People will begin to develop rashes and blisters that cannot be explained. Like the wild animals discussed in the previous paragraph, this will be widespread across the same area. Mass human casualties will also begin to occur. Many people in the same area will begin to experience nausea, disorientation, convulsions, and finally death.

There may also be odors that cannot be explained. These could range from flowery smells to pungent odors. The scent of strong garlic could even be in the air. Basically, any pronounced and unexplained odor, combined with the symptoms previously discussed could mean disaster. Another symptom may come in the form of low-lying clouds or thick fog that cannot be explained by weather conditions. In the case that national authorities are still present after such a thing happens, you may see low-flying planes spraying aerosol or liquid across your area.

Detection gear does exist to help you identify a chemical attack. Unfortunately, this equipment does not exist for biological attacks. In the case of a biological event, you must rely on your own senses. In summary, you can detect both biological and chemical attacks quite early. Simply put, it is important that you watch out for the right signs and be ready to act.

Biological Attacks: What to Do

You wake up in the middle of the night, and there's no electricity. Thunderous crashes sound from the outside. Screams echo from all the way down the street. There has been a biological attack in your town. The worst has actually happened. What do you do now?

The time has come for you to take immediate protective measures. Your first job is to ensure that the agent does not contaminate you and your loved ones. How can this be done? Members of the military will have in their possession M95 military gas masks. If you don't have one of these, you should have access to a civilian gas mask. Civilian gas masks can be purchased online for a reasonable price. You should keep one handy for each member of your family. A decent gas mask can keep you alive for at least a few hours while you work on the next steps to protect yourself from the agent. Look into different models. There are some gas masks available that house a special drinking system.

You must also understand that wearing only a protective mask will not be sufficient to keep you alive. This is precisely because chemical weapons can penetrate your skin. Suits are also available online. Performing an Internet search for biohazard suits will bring up a variety of options. It is highly suggested that you prepare before this attack takes place. Failure to do so can place you and your loved ones in harm's way.

A list is provided below. It will give you a quick overview of everything needed once the biological or chemical attack takes place. Use this as a guide to purchase the right products.

- M95 / Civilian Gask Mask (Preferably with Drinking System Installed)

- Protective Overboots
- Protective Gloves
- Biohazard Suit
- NBC Filter

These are the only items that can truly ensure your survival should a biological attack take place near you. All of these products are available for consumer purchase. I will not name brands, because I am not associated with any of the companies selling disaster preparedness products. Also, your needs are unique. You should seek out products that provide benefits that will be useful in the situations for which you want to prepare.

Contamination: What to Do

You did not act quickly enough and are now contaminated by the biological or chemical agents, so here are the steps that you need to take immediately. The most important thing here is to remove the agent from your body as quickly as possible. Firstly, do not scrape your skin. You may have been subjected to a bulk agent, which will look like droplets of thick syrupy liquid. Scraping will only spread it to other parts of your body. If you're wearing a biohazard suit, that is the only surface from which you may scrape the agent. Again, never scrape anything that is on your skin!

If nothing better is readily accessible in your case, soap and water is your best bet. Ideally, bleach would be used. You should use a precise concentration of 0.5% hypochlorite solution. For your gear, use a concentration of 5%.

Failure to decontaminate in time could be disastrous. That is why it is important to have supplies ready should this happen to you. Perhaps consider setting aside space in your pantry for these products just in case. You never know when they will come in handy. Besides, all-purpose products like soap and bleach have many uses other than decontamination. They should be a staple in your prepping pantry.

Special Note: it has been said several times in this chapter, but it cannot be said enough. Decontamination using the described methods will only work if you act quickly. This means that you should spring into action at the first sign of contamination. This may seem like common knowledge, but the truth is that there's no such thing as common knowledge when it comes to a disaster scenario. Everything is worth stating more than once.

Extended Exposure: What to Do

You have been exposed to chemical or biological agents, and you were not able to decontaminate in time; there are certain steps that you must take as quickly as possible. You will know when this time has come because you may be feeling the effects of the agent. Rest assured that there are treatment options available.

If you are still able to get to hospital, there's a good chance that they will have an antidote available. Usually, medical experts administer a special nerve agent antidote. While this does not reverse the effects of the biological or chemical agent, it does act to keep it from causing additional damage to your body. Unfortunately, this antidote is not available for consumers to purchase. It can only be obtained in a military or medical setting.

If a blood agent or a choking agent has infected you, a medical center is the only place where you can receive treatment. Even at these centers, there is little they can do for you other than keeping it from spreading further. The bad news is that many of these centers will be flooded with other people just like you looking for a cure.

Outside of a hospital setting, antibiotics will work if biological agents have infected you. The bad news is that some of these biological agents come in the form of viruses. Antibiotics do not work on viruses. In other cases, the biological weapon in question may have been modified to be resistant to antibiotics. Even still, they are your only hope. Another choice that may have positive results is Doxycycline. Civilians can procure it, and it works rather well against most biological weapons that are capable of being treated by an antibiotic. Just make sure that you consult with your doctor before stocking up on any medicines. Also respect all local and federal laws before stockpiling protective products and medicines.

You may also create a quarantine room to house anyone in your family, including yourself, who may have become infected with an agent. This will be discussed in greater detail in the following chapters.

When Pandemics Strike

If and when a pandemic strikes, you do not want to be unprepared. Being caught off-guard could potentially lead to your death and the deaths of your family members. What is a pandemic? In short, it is any infectious disease that spreads throughout entire populations spanning across large regions. This is actually already a real danger that we must worry about on a daily basis. Unfortunately, this threat could become even more of a reality in the case of a biological agent or weaponized virus being released.

The truth is that you might not always be able to leave your home and get to safety in time. Also be aware that in many cases, your local police or medical experts are not going to come to your aid. When a truly ugly pandemic strikes, you should know how to take care of your loved ones until help arrives, if it ever does. It is easy enough to simply think, "I'll put my family in the car and drive far, far away." This is not always going to be possible. In many cases, you will be stuck at home praying that your family does not become infected while the supposed experts figure out how to handle the situation.

Don't let yourself get stuck without basic knowledge that could be used to stay alive. You simply need to ask yourself one question and be prepared to act, should a biological attack become a reality. The question is quite simple:

What are you going to do when and if a pandemic hits your area? Here are a few ideas:

Quarantine Room: if you or someone you love becomes sick because of the pandemic, and you're stuck at home, you are going to need a room for quarantine purposes. This is somewhere that the infected person or persons can go to receive treatment while staying as far away from healthy people as possible.

What does a quarantine room need? Firstly, the infected person will need access to at least two to three weeks of food and water. Any good quarantine room will have storage set up for this purpose. There must also be a few other basic supplies ready for whoever is going to treat the quarantined person. Stock up on N95 masks, pain medicine, bleach, medical gloves, and strong hand sanitizer. A final important item to mention is plastic. Your quarantine room may need to be lined with thick, strong plastic in order to further facilitate the good health and continued well being of those in your home who are not yet infected.

<u>Stop the Spread of Disease</u>: if you or someone you love has been infected with a nasty disease or virus, it is important not to be careless. Cleanliness is paramount to keeping the disease from spreading to others. You should continuously wash and disinfect your hands. Also make sure never to rub your eyes or touch your face after treating the infected person. After treating someone who has become sick, your number one priority is to disinfect your own body. Do it immediately!

You should also work on keeping your immune system as strong as possible. This means that you should eat healthy and exercise. Make it your lifestyle. A strong body is one that can successfully fight off infection. One thing that many people overlook is hydration. Never allow your body to become dehydrated. Always make sure you drink the recommended amount of water each day.

Staying properly hydrated will keep you healthy, which means that you will be less susceptible to infectious diseases.

Cleanliness and sanitization should also extend to your pets. Make sure their food and water bowls are cleaned regularly. Some viruses can transfer from animals to humans. It is important to do your part to keep this from happening. It only takes a few minutes each day to sanitize your pet's food and water bowls.

Isolation: this might seem like common sense, but it is still important to mention. If a pandemic hits your area and you are stuck in your home, keep to yourself. If expert medical help arrives, that is the only exception. Keep all neighbors and anyone else who isn't a member of your immediate household away from your home. You might want to help the people around you, but there really is nothing you can do for them. The honest truth is that by inviting others into your home, you are greatly increasing the risk of someone you love becoming sick. Your only responsibility is to your household when disaster strikes.

Special Note: in the case that your local government sends notice that they are able to treat infected persons, make sure that you get to a treatment center as soon as possible. Is important to know how to take care of oneself during a disaster, but do not turn away real help if it actually exists. This is why keeping an emergency broadcast radio in your home is so important. It will allow you to listen to local emergency stations to find out what is being done to eradicate the virus.

Hunkering Down: The Basics

During a biological or chemical attack, minimizing your travel and exposure may be the smartest choice possible. It takes more than a few gallons of stored water and a hoard of ravioli cans to survive for any real length of time. Even if grocery stores are still open or groups of people are actively trading for food, you will want to have as much of what you need from your own self-sustaining methods as possible in order to minimize risk of contamination. This section is dedicated to more than just learning what you will need to survive – it is also dedicated to showing you how to make it happen.

Water

One person requires 200 gallons of water a year. To put that into perspective: that's about 5,300 personal water bottles. Food and shelter are issues that can be fudged with to a degree, but not water. If you are not under any physical stress, are in good health and are not in hot weather the longest you can survive is 3-5 days, tops. There is simply no surviving without it.

If you do not live near a body of fresh, running water or live in a climate with dependable periods of collectable rain, you are going to have to consider how to compensate for that with stored water or be able to relocate to a place that does when local services are unable to provide drinkable water and biological/chemical hazards make it dangerous to come into contact with other people.

How to Set Up Rain Water Collection

Some local governments may prohibit residents from collecting rainwater. Keep this in mind and do the research on your area's regulations so that you make informed decisions for your family. This whole setup can cost under $100, depending on regional pricing and what the demand for water collection may be at the time you decide to install the system. Tile or metal roofs will result in better quality water.

Step 1: Gather your materials. You are going to need the following:

- Water Barrel – You can buy these online, at some local stores, and can even have HUGE capacity containers built by contractors. Most barrels are available in capacities of 30 – 55 gallons.

- Enough concrete blocks to elevate the barrel from the ground, I suggest 4 or 6.

- A screen for filtering (think window screen) – This will keep bugs and debris out of your water.

- An 'S' shape aluminum downspout elbow – This will direct water into the barrel.

- 1" hose spigot with ¾" threading – This will allow you to tap into the water.

- 3/4" by 3/4" coupling

- 3/4" by 3/4" bushing

- 3/4" pipe thread with a 1" hose adapter

- 3/4" lock nut

- Metal washers

- Teflon thread tape

- Silicon caulking

Step 2: Pick a spot and prepare the base.

- Pick one of the downspouts of your home and consider that you are going to connect the "S" shape downspout elbow to it. Measure out the right distance to set up the base considering where the bottom of the elbow will lead.

- Make the location where you are installing your rainwater collection system level. You may also want to put down a bed of peat gravel, just in case your rainwater barrel overflows. Wet peat gravel is much better than mud giving way under the weight of the barrel. Set up the concrete blocks before step 3.

Step 3: Drilling and attaching

- Drill a 3/4" hole into the barrel for your spigot. Remember to drill as low as opposed to high on the barrel. Apply a circle of caulking on the inside and outside of the barrel around the hole, then attach spigot securely.

- Drill a 3/4" hole into the barrel a few inches from the top, aligned with the spigot. This is for your overflow valve. Apply a circle of caulk on the inside and outside of the barrel around the hole. Place a washer on the hose adapter, then put it through the hole from the outside. Place a washer on the threads on the inside of the barrel, apply Teflon tape and tighten with a nut. You can lead the overflow away from your home by attaching a garden hose.

Step 4: Connecting the water collection system.

- Use a hacksaw to cut the downspout about 1" below where you need it to connect with the 'S' shape elbow. Slip it into the elbow and attach tightly with screws.

- Cut out the shape of the end of the elbow into the top of the water barrel (some come with this done already) and push the downspout into the barrel. It should go at least an inch into the barrel.

Step 5: Filter.

Take a piece of screen and secure it to the part of your gutters where the water rushes down to the downspout. This will keep debris from clogging up your collection system.

Step 6: Use properly.

This water is fine as is for watering lawns, but it needs to be boiled before human consumption. If you have composite roof tiles, those chemicals will be present in your water. Plan on switching out your full water barrels every six months or so, otherwise it will start to taste off. Treat using iodine or another approved water purification method if you plan on drinking the water you collect.

Sustenance

There are lots of great reasons why families are growing their own foods and stocking emergency pantries. Cutting down on costs and enjoying nature is one reason, but being able to depend on yourself is extremely important when a bio attack or pandemic make going shopping a very bad idea. Even if you cannot grow any of your own produce, you can make sure that your family has enough food stored to comfortably survive for a year while cut off from supermarkets.

Each adult is going to need the following amount of each food group to survive for a period of one year: 400 lbs. of grains, 90 lbs. of beans/legumes, 90 lbs. of fruits and vegetables, 75lbs. of dairy, 20lbs meat protein (add that unto beans for vegetarians), 60 lbs. sugar and 20 lbs. oil. This is based on about a 2000-calorie diet.

Consider all of the vitamins that your body needs when deciding what foods to put into your pantry. Remember that scurvy used to be a very prominent problem not that long ago, so keep vitamins as well as foodstuffs in your emergency pantry.

Grains: Rice, oatmeal packets, puffed wheat cereal and flour all fall into this category. Make sure that the containers are unopened or vacuum sealed. Keep the area dry and periodically check the storage area for damp spots. Without carbohydrates, your body will quickly decide that it is starving and organs may begin to shut down.

Beans/Legumes: These are a no-brainer because of how high in protein they are and how cheap they can be. You will also need the fiber to keep your digestive system regular in times of high stress. If sickness is rampant, you may not have the luxury of seeing a doctor for intestinal distress. Keep beans dry and away from moisture, or they will start to sprout.

Fruits and vegetables: Finding these in cans is extremely easy. Consider getting preserves as well as fruit cocktail. Do not underestimate how important fruits are going to be when you are stuck in your home. Canned fruits and vegetables are superior to frozen in this situation because of how unstable utilities may be during a pandemic.

Dairy: Powdered milk and containers of milk alternatives (almond milk, soy milk, etc.) that do not require refrigeration would work best. You can use this in creating sauces and baking. Do not consider it a drink for when you are thirsty in place of water. You are going to need it for its nutritional purposes. Stick to water whenever possible for your thirst.

Meat Protein: Simply put, you may get sick of nothing but beans and could probably use a break from all that fiber. Meat jerky and cured ham are perfect examples of what can fall into this category.

Sugar and Oil: You are better off storing actual sugar than sugary treats. You can use the sugar to sweeten drinks, grains or bake cakes. Sometimes you may just feel that your insulin level is dipping too low and can use a spoonful. You are also far less likely to eat through bags of sugar right away than you are snack cakes when you are stuck at home. The same goes for oil. Store containers of vegetable and olive oil for food preparation rather than greasy snacks.

Additional Sustenance Recommendations

Water additives: Consider adding water flavoring packets or liquid flavor drops to your pantry. In the event that you have to switch to well water or purify rainwater for consumption, these flavor additives can help hide unpleasant tastes. If you purify your water with iodine, do not add any flavoring until at least an hour has passed since purification. It can otherwise interact with the iodine's ability to kill bacteria.

Salt: Most of the food in your pantry will already have some form of sodium from the canning or preserving process. However, salt is considered a luxury item and can be traded for things that you need. It is required for curing meats; so having salt on hand indirectly means that you can also add meat to your stores by going hunting. This underappreciated spice makes foods palatable and cannot be easily replenished.

Coffee: While coffee has no practical use in staying alive, it can make a difference and help you stay alert at times when sleep is a luxury. People are also in love with the addictive and bitter-tasting brown beverage. Because it is so hard to replenish, other people may be willing to trade coffee for things that you need.

Nicotine Products: Consider keeping a couple of boxes of cigarettes sealed up and put away for possible trading purposes. Keep them in a dry place and double bag them in plastic baggies if you do not care for the smell. Even if you are highly stressed, do not use them yourself, nicotine is highly addictive and you may end up trading away things that you need to other preppers in order to indulge in one more cigarette. They are also terrible for respiratory ailments, and breathing clearly may be an issue during a bio attack or pandemic.

Local Threats

Any number of scenarios could occur that would require you to protect your family. In the case of a major disaster, there will be several types of people looking to take what you have built up for your own survival needs. Let's examine these people further:

- <u>People in Need </u>– These are individuals or families who are normally good, but have been driven by a desire to provide for their loved ones. There is a very good chance that you will encounter many people from this category when the worst happens. Be wary of them and willing to protect your property, family, and supplies.

- <u>Terrorists</u> – This category is for anyone whose primary intention is to harm others. It used to be that we only had to worry about extremists in major disaster scenarios; that is simply not true anymore. They are out there, and you must be ready for them.

- Professional Criminals – These people are likely the number two threat (the first being people in need) you will face in terms of home defense. They thrive on chaos; it helps them nefariously acquire goods without worrying about whether or not they'll be caught by law enforcement. Always be wary of anyone who attempts to make face-to-face contact with you during an emergency situation. Their intentions could be innocent in nature, but do you want to take that chance? If you are dealing with someone you don't trust, turn him or her away.

The unfortunate truth is that you will encounter people from the first category in your neighborhood or town. These are waiters and waitresses you have seen in local cafes. They are your acquaintances, neighbors, teachers, salesmen, or basically anyone who does not live under your roof. If you are well prepared, there is a good chance that you have enough supplies to keep your immediate family clothed and fed for at least a few months. Did you store enough food, water, and medical supplies for the whole city? You will have to be prepared to turn these people away. They might seem innocent enough; they probably are. They aren't your responsibility, and given the chance, these people will resort to extreme measures to take what isn't already theirs.

While it is true that each category of people must be dealt with in a different way, they can ALL be considered immediate threats to your continued survival. If you decide to help someone outside of your circle of trust, make sure that your generosity does not place your loved ones into harm's way.

Know Your Rights

The United States is a place where citizens who respect the law are able to defend their homes and property. We are granted the right to possess weapons for the purpose of self-defense. The Second Amendment is in place to ensure this very thing. With a select few important restrictions, Americans may own many different types of firearms. This includes handguns and rifles. Assault rifles and explosive devices typically require licensure and are quite controlled in nature.

If you are the head of your household, it is your great responsibility to protect your family and property. Should you choose to own one or more firearms, it is important to take reasonable measures. For instance, try not to go overboard. Decide what is needed to exercise your rights as the protector of your home if extreme circumstances arise and go with that number. Also remember that your choice to own weaponry is no different from your neighbor's choice to be a pacifist. All should respect both ways of life.

Weapons

For those people thinking about purchasing a firearm, here are some pros and cons:

- <u>Handguns</u> – Easy to conceal; great stopping power; may be handled with ease by women; fantastic at close range. Unfortunately, low caliber models have reduced stopping power, and the range of most handguns is rather limited.

- <u>Rifles</u> – Small caliber models can be handled by women; fantastic accuracy and range; great stopping power. These weapons cannot be concealed and are prone to being taken away from you by an attacker.

- <u>Shotguns</u> – Shotguns have remarkable stopping power and can be intimidating when brandished, but they are not concealable; capacity is limited. These weapons are also prone to being taken from you by your attacker.

Always respect gun laws in your area! Make sure to practice proper gun safety measures at all times. This includes keeping your firearms locked in a gun safe. Never store your guns where children can gain access to them! Some gun owners argue that safely stored weapons are not readily accessible in the case of an emergency, but there should be no exceptions made in a household with children.

One final note about gun ownership – There's a study floating around that claims a gun in your home will cause you to be forty-three times more susceptible to accidental shootings or suicides with the weapon in question. You should know that the results of any study will always be skewed toward the standings of the persons or organization conducting it. This particular study's results were actually improperly presented, causing the conclusions not to be drawn fairly. If you are still on the fence about owning a firearm, be sure to seek out as much information from both sides of the argument as possible. Drawn your own conclusions. Just remember, you are the head of the household; it is your job to protect your family, regardless of the results of inconclusive data presented in a skewed manner.

Other Home Defense Weapons

It must be mentioned that virtually anything can be turned into a weapon and used for defensive purposes. If you are not able to gain access to a firearm, rest assured that you have plenty of other options.

The following list should give you some good ideas. Again, if you begin collecting weapons for home defense now, please respect your local laws and ordinances.

- <u>Machetes</u> – this is both an excellent tool and formidable weapon. The machete is typically used for cutting, as well as opening and breaking a variety of different things. You can cut firewood, metal cans, rope, and even windows. It is a must-have for any survivalist.

- <u>Axes</u> – An axe is another fantastic weapon and tool that can use for home defense and survivalist purposes. Most people who abuse the next in their lifetime know that it is the next best thing to a machete that you can have in your collection. It can be used to chop wood, and break through countless objects and obstacles.

- <u>Crowbars</u> – One great thing about crowbar is that it never goes dull, because it has no sharp edges. Is made of heavy steel, which means it will never break. Its shape makes it perfect for prying open doors and windows, climbing, and it holds its own as a striking weapon. Finally, a crowbar can be used to reach for things that are too high up, such as ladders that you're not touch the ground.

- <u>Baseball Bats</u> – there are a few cons to using baseball bats for home defense. The first is that wooden bats are easy to break and splinter after having been used it a few times. Aluminum bats content over time. Still, they make a fantastic backup weapon for defensive purposes. Should you find yourself without a weapon, a baseball bat hiding in the corner can be a godsend.

- <u>Shovels</u> – this is both a great tool and a last resort weapon that your attacker might not expect you to use. This item can be used to hold attackers back at arms length, and you might even be able to fend off some attackers with it. They will focus to swing to produce devastating effects, especially if you sharpen the point.

There are many more items that can be utilized for home protection. Some of them might be lying around your house right now. The point of this list is to show that weapons of both the traditional and non-traditional variety can be used to protect your loved ones should the worst happen. While this book is focused on how to survive a biological attack, things such as home defense must be taken into account in any scenario.

When all hell breaks loose in your town, one of the first things that you need to look into is how to protect your family and property. While many of us don't like to think about the possibility of fending off our neighbors, it can become a real possibility when disaster strikes.

The best thing about many of these weapons is that they can be used when you're forced to hunker down, as well as when you are forced out of your home and into the wilderness. Protecting yourself on the run is just as important as keeping safe at home. In the event of a biological attack, survivors are going to be scrambling to take what they can, even if that means taking things from other people. Take the necessary precautions to keep this from happening to you. Even a small concealed knife can make all the difference between an extra day of survival or sudden death at the hands of someone you might not have considered a threat mere weeks ago.

Customizing Your Bug Out Bag

When SHTF, you might not be able to stay at home. In fact, there is high probability that you might just need to get the heck out of Dodge. If this happens to you after a biological or chemical attack, and you have not been infected, all the long-term home storage in the world won't save you for what might come next. Depending on the size of your family, you will need a bug out bag with some important things stored in it. This bag should be easily carried or strapped onto your body. It should also be made of durable materials to help it withstand the elements and extended rough travel.

Many companies offer pre-packaged survival kits, and some of these products might work well for your needs. Of these pre-packaged kits, the "survival bucket" seems to be the most popular. These are basically 72-hour emergency kits that come in a handy bucket. In this chapter, we won't focus on those. The items stored in a bug out bag must meet the unique needs of your specific family and situation. The good news is that obtaining many of these things is a relatively cheap endeavor. A lot of the items needed for your bug out bag are common sense things such as food, water, and medical supplies.

In the following pages, I'll go over some of the most popular and useful things that you might want to take into consideration. Just know that this isn't an exhaustive list; after all, your needs could be completely different, which means you will have to plan accordingly. This is merely a list of suggestions that will go a long way in keeping you and family from facing more difficulties than are necessary, should the worst happen.

One final point worth mentioning: Don't buy a bug out bag until you have acquired all the supplies that will fill it. You will have a much easier time this way.

Bug Out Bag: Medical Supplies

- 2 Pairs of Disposable Medical Gloves
- 6 Compact Packs of Tissues
- 2 Small First Aid Kits
- Portable Lancing Device
- Allergy Tablets (such as Benadryl)
- 1 Bottle (NSAID) Anti-Inflammatory Drug (Naproxen Sodium, Acetaminophen)
- Portable Sewing Kit & Spools of Strong Thread
- 1 Tube Antibiotic Cream
- Mylar Blankets
- Insect Repellant
- Bee Sting Kit
- Medications for Food Allergies

Note: Make sure that your first aid kits have an ample supply of bandages, medical tape, and gauze. Also consider purchasing a first aid kit that comes with tweezers, a tool that will prove indispensible in no time.

Your medical supplies may differ from this list if you suffer from ailments that require regular treatment, such as daily injections.

Bug Out Bag: Food & Water

- 15 Protein Bars
- Water Bottles (collapsible)
- Metal Canteens
- 4 Liters of Clean Drinking Water
- 40 - 50 Water Purification Tablets
- Small Can Opener
- Small Metal Cook Pot
- Several Sporks
- 5 Containers of MRE (dehydrated meals)
- Portable Stove & Fuel
- Elastic Sports Bandages

Note: Having enough drinking water for your family is the difference between life and death. Keep the *"one gallon of water per person, per day"* formula in mind when determining how much drinking water your family will need. Aside from the drinking water mentioned in the above list, consider setting aside a few gallons purified drinking water to go alongside your bug out bag. Just make sure you can carry everything if it comes down to it. If you must travel light, one liter of water per day, per person is the absolute minimum you will need.

Once your drinking water runs out (it probably will within 24 hours), you are going to need to know how to purify any future water that you find and gather. That's where the extra tablets come in. My book, *Stay Alive*, goes into further detail about water purification methods.

Bug Out Bag: Hygiene & Bedding

- Small Bottle of Hand Sanitizer
- 1 Bar of Camping Soap
- Travel Toilet Paper
- 10 Plastic Bags
- 1 Small Mirror (useful for hygiene and signaling purposes)
- Travel-Sized Shampoo
- 2 Packs of Toilet Chemicals
- 1 Tube Tent
- 1 Tarp
- 1 Bedroll per person
- Wool Blankets (these can be rolled into the bedroll for easier storage)

Bug Out Bag: Defense & Survival Tools

- Firearm
- Ammunition (at least 30 rounds)
- Survival Knife
- Pepper Spray
- Collapsible Baton
- Handcuffs
- Binoculars
- Snare Wire
- Portable Hand Saw
- Machete

Note: Be wise when choosing a survival knife. The one you choose will be based on your specific needs and the region in which you live. There are many different configurations offered, so research them all and choose carefully.

Bug Out Bag: Clothing and Miscellaneous

- 4 Plastic Ponchos
- Durable Socks (ALWAYS keep your feet dry)
- Undergarments
- Convertible Pants
- Extra Long-Sleeved Shirts
- N95 Face Masks
- Solar Radio
- Duct Tape
- Nylon Cord (about 50 – 60 feet)
- Waterproof Matches
- 2 Pairs of Work Gloves
- 5-Hour Emergency Candles
- 1 Police Whistle
- Sturdy Bandana
- Fishing Kits
- Non-Lubricated Condoms (for additional water storage)
- Cell Phone

- Solar Charger
- Mini LED Flashlights
- Plenty of Batteries
- Glowsticks
- Tinderbox

Predicting Weather Without Modern Equipment

Having a true connection with nature can make a huge difference in terms of survival. Knowing which signs are important to look for and finding them simply by scanning the horizon can help you understand weather conditions without the need for gadgets. In truth, most survival scenarios will involve a lack of modern technology, so it is wise to understand what to look for when the only tool that you have to predict the weather is nature itself. If you manage to survive a biological attack, you might find it necessary to leave your home in search of safer ground. If this happens, it is important to understand how the weather actually works.

It's actually very simple to forecast the weather simply by knowing what to look out for. The truly great thing about nature is that it is always giving us signs, and when you are aware of what they are and how to find them, you can better prepare for whichever weather conditions happen to come your way. Firstly, cloud watching and even smelling the air are very important techniques for natural weather forecasting. There are also some other methods that can be utilized. For instance, if you spot a red sky during sunset while looking west, this is a telltale sign of a high-pressure system with dry air moving in. The red sky is actually a stirring of dust particles that happen to be in the air. Seeing the same red sky to the east means that the dry air is moving out of your area.

Following is a list of some other things that you can look out for to get a better idea of how to forecast the weather without fancy tools.

<u>Cloud Watching</u> - keeping an eye on the various cloud formations is an extremely important part of predicting possible weather conditions in your area. For example, if you spot complete cloud cover on a winter night, you can expect warmer weather ahead. This is because blankets of clouds typically keep away heat radiation that serves to lower temperatures when the sky is clear. *Cumulus* towers denote the possibility of rain showers at some point in the day. Separate cloud layers that seem to be moving in opposite directions typically mean that hail or other bad weather conditions are coming. *Cirrus* clouds warn of bad weather arriving within 24 hours. *Cumulonimbus* cloud formations (they look eerily similar to atomic bomb clouds) denote severe weather. Finally, a *Mammatus* cloud formation is a sign that current severe weather conditions are dissipating.

Above: Cumulus clouds are a sign that rain may be on the way later the same day.

Above: Mammatus clouds are a sign of dangerous weather dissipating.

Above: Cumulonimbus clouds denote severe weather is incoming.

Above: The appearance of a circle around the moon means that humidity is rising and you can expect rain the next day.

Above: Cirrus clouds fly ahead of severe weather storms.

<u>Moon Watching</u> - if you spot a ring around the moon, this is an indication that rain will come within the next several days. In extremely cold conditions, it also means that snow is on the way. A sign that a significant amount of dust is in the air is a reddish or pale moon. A bright and sharp looking moon denotes that a low-pressure system is about to sweep through your area.

<u>Wind</u> – An easterly blowing wind indicates that a storm is approaching. Westerly blowing winds indicate the exact opposite. Deciduous trees actually display the underside of their leaves when unusual winds approach. This is typically because they develop in a way that keeps those leaves right side up during normal winds.

<u>Smelling Air</u> – one of the first things that should be known about the air around you is

that plants actually release waste in low-pressure atmospheres. This can create a smell that is very similar to compost, which actually indicates that rain is coming. If you live near a swamp, you may already know that they release gas just before storms come. This is typically due to the lower pressure of storms. This creates an unpleasant smell, which is a fantastic warning sign. Finally, flowers tend to have a stronger scent just before rainy weather approaches.

Humidity - It is quite true that many people can feel the humidity in the air; this is especially true of people with long hair. The more humid the environment, the quicker hair can become frizzy and even curled in some instances. This is also true with the leaves of trees. If your area has oak or maple trees, their leaves actually curl in high humidity. This typically precedes extremely heavy rain or storms. Pinecone scales usually remain closed if there is high humidity. The scales typically open in dry air. Finally, wood always swells when the air is humid. Salt will also clump.

Above: How your hair behaves from day to day is a direct indication of humidity. The frizzier it is, the more humidity exists in the air. Waves of humidity often precipitate wet weather systems.

<u>Grass</u> - Keeping an eye on the grass around you can also tell you a lot about the weather. For example, if the grass around you is dry, this is an indication of clouds or powerful breezes, which in itself is an indication of rain. If dew has formed on the grass, it likely will not rain all day.

Above: Morning dew on grass is an indicator of calm winds and suggests that no new weather fronts will blow in that day.

<u>Animal Watching</u> – watching the animals around you can also help immensely. Keep an eye on birds, cows, cats, and even turtles for a good indication of what the weather will be like throughout the day. If the birds around you are flying rather high in the sky, the weather will likely be fair. When a low-pressure system is on the way, birds will tend to keep lower to the ground. This is typically because oncoming storms can cause some discomfort in the ears of avian creatures.

Some birds will actually take refuge just before a storm arrives. Other animals become very quiet just before a storm or strong rain. If you have cows around you, watch their habits throughout the day. They usually lie down just before a thunderstorm arrives. If other bad weather conditions are imminent, they usually gather closely together. Anthills are also great indications of the weather. If you see anthills being built with extremely steep sides, there's a good chance that rain is on the way.

One final thing that you can do is to build a small campfire outside. Watch the smoke that rises from the campfire. Is it rising steadily? If not, look to see if the smoke is swirling. If it swirls and then descends, a low-pressure system is coming soon.

Knowing what the weather will be like on any given day will help you dictate how to proceed when you are forced to travel or live in nature for any amount of time.

BONUS SECTION

SURVIVAL HERBS

Bonus Section: Survival Herbs

While many of us may think our stockpiled medical supplies will be enough to sustain us when there are no more hospitals or even doctors left to treat our injuries, that couldn't be further from the truth. In reality, even the best preppers out there may only have supplies enough to last a year or two in a disaster scenario. The good news is that there are plenty of medicinal options available in the way of herbs. Natural healing methods have been in practice since the dawn of mankind, and they continue to be viable methods of treatment even in the modern world. When disaster strikes, you should know what to gather and how to prepare it. This is knowledge that could save the lives of you and your loved ones.

My previous book, Stay Alive, covered some of the basic medicinal herbs. The section you are reading now will go into much more detail. Here you will learn what to gather, how to prepare it, and what it can do for you. While there are many more herbs out there that provide a wealth of health benefits, covered here are the ones that directly benefit survivalists.

Herbal Medicine: Circulation

Gotu Kola *Centella asiatica*

To improve leg circulation, pour 2 cups of boiling water over 1 teaspoon of gotu kola herb. Steep for at least 10 minutes and drink 2 cups per day.

Turmeric *Curcuma longa*

When dealing with fresh turmeric, wear gloves or be prepared for your hands to be stained by its natural juice. To prepare your own turmeric powder, you will need to wash and boil the roots of the plant until soft (about 40 minutes). Set them out in the sun or next to a kitchen fire to dry for a day or two. When the roots are completely dried out (they should be shriveled), they can be ground into powder.

Just 1 teaspoon of turmeric powder mixed into 1 cup of warm milk, when taken 3 times a day, can radically improve circulation.

Above: An artistic and accurate depiction of the flower, leaves, stem and roots of the turmeric plant.

Herbal Medicine: Chest Colds & Respiratory Ailments

<u>Garlic</u> *Allium sativum*

Bronchitis and lung infections can benefit from taking homemade garlic syrup. To make the medicinal syrup, chop up 8 garlic cloves and place into a jar. Cover chopped garlic with 8 tablespoons of honey. Allow the mixture to stand for several days while the honey becomes infused with garlic's medicinal nutrients. Strain out the garlic and administer 1 teaspoon to children and 4 teaspoons to adults. This can be done daily to boost the immune system as well as treat any infections.

Infants suffering from fevers or croup can take 1-2 teaspoons of garlic milk every 4 hours for relief. To make garlic milk, thinly slice 3 garlic cloves and boil with 2 cups of milk (the type of milk, dairy or nut, does not matter) and boil on low for about 20 minutes. If you cannot store leftover garlic milk in a cool place, a new batch must be made for the next dose.

Licorice *Glycyrrhiza glabra*

Washed roots and bark may be chewed directly for some relief of chest congestion. A tea can be very beneficial and soothing as well. To make licorice tea, combine 1/4-cup ground licorice root with 2 cups water. Bring to a boil for 10-12 minutes.

Mustard *Brassica nigra*

Relieve symptoms of chest congestion by creating mustard poultice. Add a small amount of water to mustard powder (or freshly crushed pods and seeds) to create a paste. Spread the paste on a piece of cloth and place cloth-side-down on chest. Remove if there is any skin irritation present.

Herbal Medicine: Insect Bites & Stings

Aloe *Aloe vera*

Can be applied to bites and stings to reduce swelling and irritation. Cut a piece of the leaf off and apply the gel directly to the affected area.

Cedar *Cedrus deodara*

Create a natural and effective insect repellent by combining 10 drops of cedar oil and 1 tablespoon of vegetable oil. Caution: Pregnant women should take extra care not to ingest any cedar oil.

Marigold Petals *Calendula officinalis*

These petals can be used to treat bee stings. Boil 3 flowers in a cup of water. Allow the flowers to infuse for 15 minutes. For quick results, drink a cup every 3 – 4 hours until symptoms lessen. DO NOT confuse this plant with French or African marigolds, which should NEVER be ingested.

Marshmallow *Althea officinalis*

Crush the roots into a powder and add just enough cold water to mix into a paste. Apply thickly to affected area and allow to dry. Redo the application every 3 hours.

Plantain Leaves

Use moist and macerated leaves on insect bites. After the leaf has dried, remove and apply another moist leaf.

Sage Leaves

These should be macerated before applying. Sage can be used on scorpion stings & spider bites.

Witch Hazel *Hamamelis virginiana*

This is best used on mosquito bites. Cut a 1-oz piece of bark and simmer it in 500ml of water for 10 – 15 minutes. Strain the liquid into a container and let it cool for 2 hours.

Above: Sage plants have thick, soft-feeling leaves.

Herbal Medicine: Joint Pain

Cat's Claw *Uncaria tomentosa*

Painful inflammation related to arthritis and joint pain can be calmed by drinking cat's claw tea. Make the tea by combing 2 teaspoons of crushed cat's claw bark with 1 cup of water, boil, steep for 10-15 minutes and strain. Drink up to 3 times a day. Do not administer to pregnant women or children.

Cayenne Pepper *Capsicum annuum*

For the external treatment joint pain combine 1/2 teaspoon of powder or fresh purée to 1-cup warm vegetable oil. Rub the warm mixture on the affected area for symptom relief. Caution: Do not administer cayenne to children less than two years old.

Mustard *Brassica nigra*

Combine 1 part mustard oil with 40 parts alcohol to create a pain-relieving lotion.

Caution: Do not allow undiluted mustard oil come into contact with the skin, irritation may occur.

Herbal Medicine: Oral Health

<u>Cloves</u> *Eugenia caryophyllata*

Fight tooth decay and numb tooth and gum pain with clove oil. Just dab a few drops on the affected area. To make clove oil, take dried clove flower buds and place them in a small container. Pour a very small amount of olive oil over them (just enough to cover them slightly) and let them stand over at least 1 week. The longer the clove flowers steep in the oil, the more powerful the clove oil will be. Strain the mixture before use.

<u>Myrrh</u> *Commiphora myrrha*

Sore gums and cold sores can be easily and quickly treated with the sap from this tall bush. Collect the resin that forms in the cracks of the bark - it is well known for its antiseptic properties – and can be directly applied to the affected area.

<u>Yarrow</u> *Achillea millefolium*

Fresh roots may be washed and immediately chewed on to relieve toothaches. Pregnant women should avoid ingesting yarrow in large doses.

Above: Yarrow plant with flowers.

Herbal Medicine: Stomach Ailments

<u>Bayberry</u> *Myrica cerifera*

When you run out of the pink stuff, diarrhea can be cured with this tasty tea. To prepare a gargling decoction, put 1 teaspoon of bark into 1-cup cold water into a pot and bring to a boil. Allow to sit and steep for 5-10 minutes (the longer, the more potent). Drink no more than 3 times a day. Gargling this tea before drinking it will add the additional benefit of soothing sore throats.

<u>Coriander</u> *Coriandrum sativum*

Those who suffer from indigestion can benefit from this coriander-infused tea: Bruise 1 teaspoon of coriander seeds (place them in a bag and beat them around, but do not crush them). You can also use 1/ teaspoon of prepared powder. Place herb in a cup and pour 1 cup boiled water on top. Steep for 5 minutes. Drink after meals, up to 3 cups per day. Caution: Pregnant women should avoid ingesting coriander in high doses.

Above left to right: Coriander flowers with stems and leaves and seeds.

<u>Marshmallow</u> *Althea officinalis*

Treat acid stomach, heartburn and irritable bowel conditions by drinking 3 cups of marshmallow water daily. Soak 1 ounce (about 1/8 of a cup) of sliced root in 3-4 cups of cold water overnight.

Above: Marshmallow flowers and buds.

Senna *Cassia angustifolia*

Make a laxative for adults by steeping 6-12 pods in 4-5 tablespoons water. Children and the elderly may have the laxative made from steeping 3-4 pods in 4-5 tablespoons water. Additionally, steeping 3-1/2 ounces senna leaves, 1/2-teaspoon coriander, 1/2-teaspoon ginger and 1 quart of boiling water for 15 minutes can make a powerful laxative drink.

Above: Senna plant with blooming flowers.

Herbal Medicine: Aches and Pains

<u>Bayberry</u> *Myrica cerifera*

Sore throats can be soothed by gargling with this herb. To prepare a gargling decoction, put 1 teaspoon of bark into 1-cup cold water into a pot and bring to a boil. Allow tea to sit and steep for 5-10 minutes (the longer, the more potent). While gargling with it will greatly ease sore throats, drinking it will also help any digestive issues, especially diarrhea.

Above: Ripe bayberries with stems and leaves attached

Pennywort *Umbilicus rupestris*

This earache treatment is so effective that you should consider using it instead of OTC medication whether available or not. Collect the round leaves of this plant and crush them until a green juice is made. Take a few drops of the juice (at body temperature) and place them in the ear. Plug it up with a cotton ball.

Above: Pennywort's leaves are round and a little disc-shaped.

Ginger *Zingiber officinalis*

Sufferers of painful menstrual cramps can soothe the pain by drinking a cup of warm ginger tea. To make tea, grate 2 tablespoons of ginger root and place in a cup. Pour 1 cup of boiling water on top. Allow tea to steep for 5 minutes. Limit intake to 1 cup per day. A higher dose of ginger may bring on a menses cycle. Caution: Do not use if pregnant or if high fever, ulcer or bleeding are present.

Valerian *Valeriana officinalis*

This ancient remedy was popular among Romans. The roots of this herb must be dried, peeled and dehydrated. Pound into powder and you can make an excellent pain-relief tea that also soothes stress and helps with insomnia. To make the tea, combine 3 teaspoons of valerian root powder with 2/3-cups hot water. Let mixture steep for 5-15 minutes, then drain and drink warm. Drink up to 3 cups a day and make sure to drink one of them before bedtime.

Above from left to right: Valerian leaves, flowering buds and roots.

JD Everman

Thank you for reading Surviving Doomsday!

If you like the book, please consider leaving an honest review!

Title: Surviving Doomsday